Grammar Rules!

Tanya Gibb

NSW Edition

Name: ______________________________

Class: ______________________________

Grammar Rules! Student Book 1
NSW Edition
ISBN: 978 0 6550 9241 4

Publisher: Catherine Charles-Brown
Designer and typesetter: Trish Hayes
Illustrator: Stephen Michael King
Series editor: Marie James
Indigenous consultant: Al Fricker

This edition published in 2023 by Matilda Education Australia, an imprint of Meanwhile Education Pty Ltd
Melbourne, Australia
T: 1300 277 235
E: customersupport@matildaed.com.au
www.matildaeducation.com.au

First edition published in 2008 by Macmillan Science and Education Australia Pty Ltd

Publication data
Author: Tanya Gibb
Title: *Grammar Rules! Student Book 1 NSW Edition*
ISBN: 978 0 6550 9241 4

A catalogue record for this book is available from the National Library of Australia

Printed in China by Central
Sep-2022

Contents

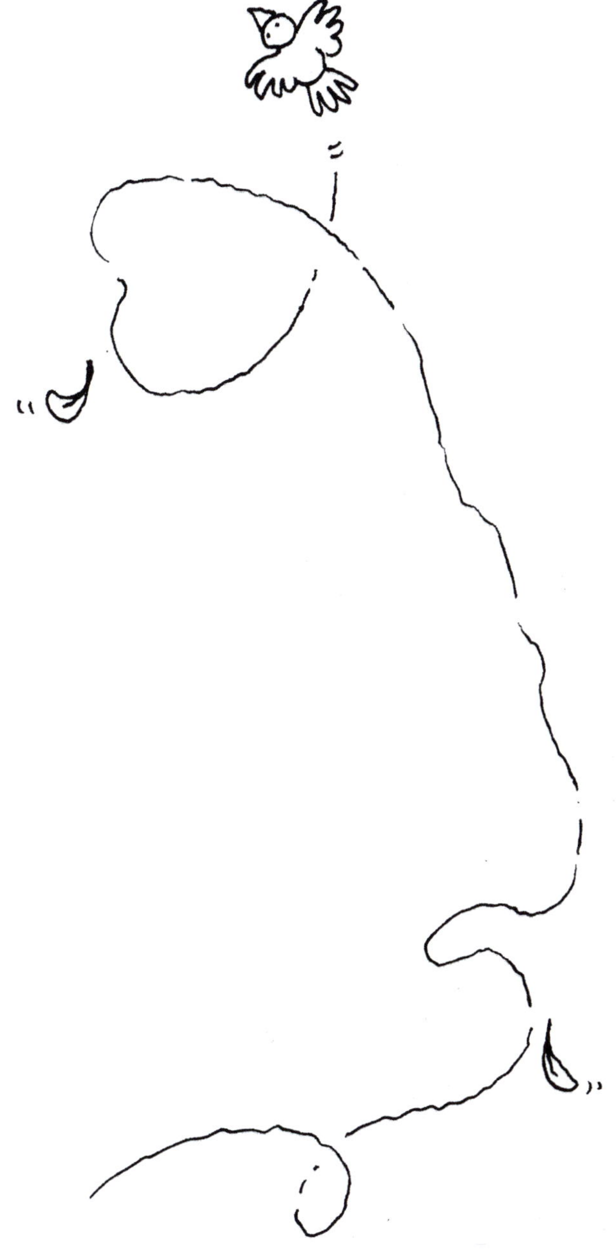

Note to Teachers and Parents

Grammar Rules!

Grammar Rules! comprehensively meets the requirements of the 2021 NSW Education Standards Authority **English K–2 Syllabus**, which states that "through practice and experience in understanding and creating texts, students learn about the power, purpose, value and art of English for communication, knowledge and enjoyment" (p15). *Grammar Rules!* also supports implementation of **Australian Curriculum English**, V9, 2022.

The **NSW English K–2 Syllabus** recognises that knowledge and understanding of grammar at the level of the whole text and at the level of the sentence, clause, phrase or word, underpins students' comprehension of oral and written texts, and their ability to create effective texts for various purposes and audiences.

Grammar Rules! provides a conceptually sound, scope and sequence of context-based activities that support teaching and learning in English. Although the title for the series is *Grammar Rules!*, the series in not just about grammar. Each unit of work in the series begins at the level of the whole text by identifying purpose and audience for the model text, providing teaching opportunities to activate students' background knowledge of the topic or the text type, and then supporting students in reading comprehension. The texts provided can be used for discussion of text forms and features and sentence structures, as well as for vocabulary expansion. The texts can also be used as models for students to use when creating their own written, spoken or multimodal texts. The texts included in *Grammar Rules!* cover a variety of informative, imaginative and persuasive texts and hybrid texts that use elements of different types of texts.

Grammar Rules! also teaches the conventions of punctuation and some aspects of spelling (for example, plural nouns, homophones and compound words); literary elements such as onomatopoeia, rhyme and alliteration; and the way visual elements function to support or construct meaning. Other areas of the **English K–2 Syllabus** covered in *Grammar Rules!* include critical reading and reflecting on character, setting and plot in narrative texts (literature).

Student Book 1

Units of work

Student Book 1 contains 35 weekly units of work presented in a conceptually sound scope and sequence. The intention is for students to work through the units in the sequence in which they are presented. See the **Scope and Sequence Chart** on pages 6–7 for more information. There are also regular Revision Units that can be used for consolidation or assessment purposes.

The sample texts in *Student Book 1* are not tied to any particular content across other curriculum areas. This allows teachers and students to focus on the way language is structured in the different types of texts according to purpose and audience. Students can then use this knowledge to critically evaluate, respond to and create texts in other learning areas.

Icons

Encourages students to create texts of their own to demonstrate their understanding of the text structures and features taught in the unit. These activities focus on written language; however, many also provide opportunities for using spoken language to engage with others, make presentations and develop skills in using ICT.

Highlights useful grammatical rules and concepts. The rule is always introduced the first time students need it to complete an activity.

Tells students that a special hint is provided for an activity. It might be a tip about language functions, or a reminder to look at a rule in a previous unit.

Encourages students to assess their progress across each unit.

Grammar Rules! Glossary

A valuable glossary is provided at the end of *Student Book 1*. Teachers and students can use this as a straightforward dictionary of grammar terminology, or as a summary of important grammar rules used in *Student Book 1*. Page references are also given for the point in the book where the rule was first introduced, so that students can go back to that unit if they need more information or further revision of the rule.

Grammar Rules! Student Book 1 (ISBN 9780655092414) © Tanya Gibb/Matilda Education Australia

Pull-Out Writing Log

At the centre of *Student Book 1* is a practical pull-out Writing Log so that students can keep track of the texts they have created or attempted to create. The Writing Log also includes a handy reminder of the writing process, as well as a checklist of types of texts for students to try.

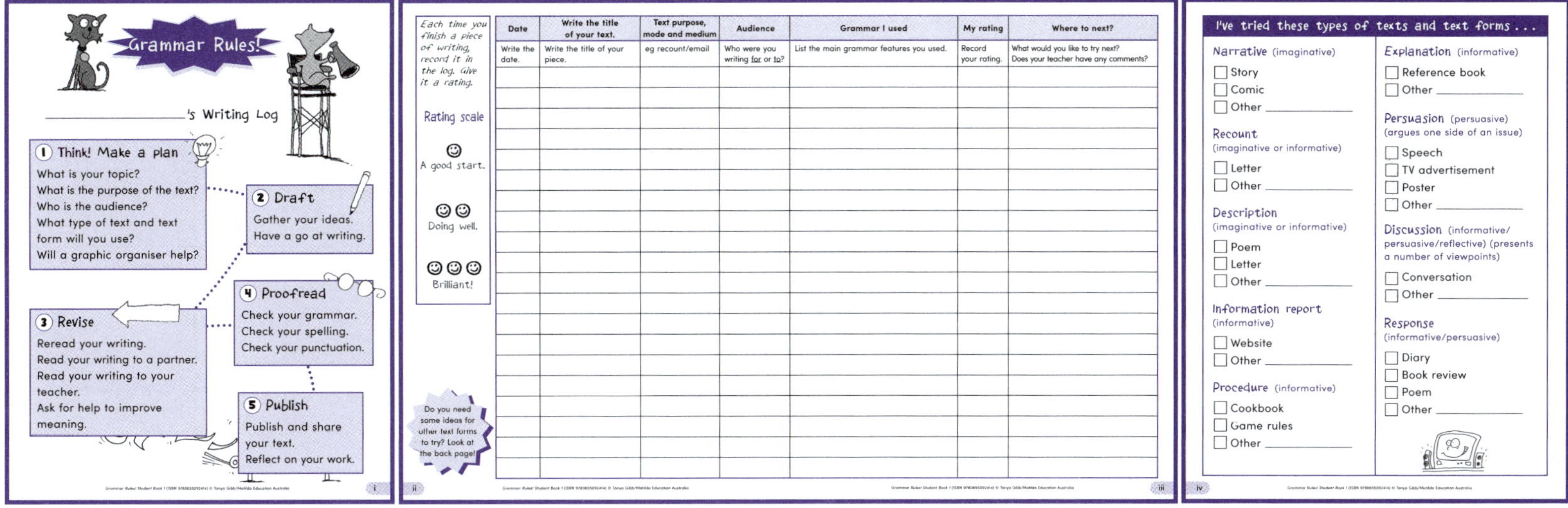

Date	Write the title of your text.	Text purpose, mode and medium	Audience	Grammar I used	My rating	Where to next?
Write the date.	Write the title of your piece.	eg recount/email	Who were you writing for or to?	List the main grammar features you used.	Record your rating.	What would you like to try next? Does your teacher have any comments?

I've tried these types of texts and text forms . . .

Narrative (imaginative)
- Story
- Comic
- Other ________

Recount (imaginative or informative)
- Letter
- Other ________

Description (imaginative or informative)
- Poem
- Letter
- Other ________

Information report (informative)
- Website
- Other ________

Procedure (informative)
- Cookbook
- Game rules
- Other ________

Explanation (informative)
- Reference book
- Other ________

Persuasion (persuasive) (argues one side of an issue)
- Speech
- TV advertisement
- Poster
- Other ________

Discussion (informative/persuasive/reflective) (presents a number of viewpoints)
- Conversation
- Other ________

Response (informative/persuasive)
- Diary
- Book review
- Poem
- Other ________

Unit at a glance

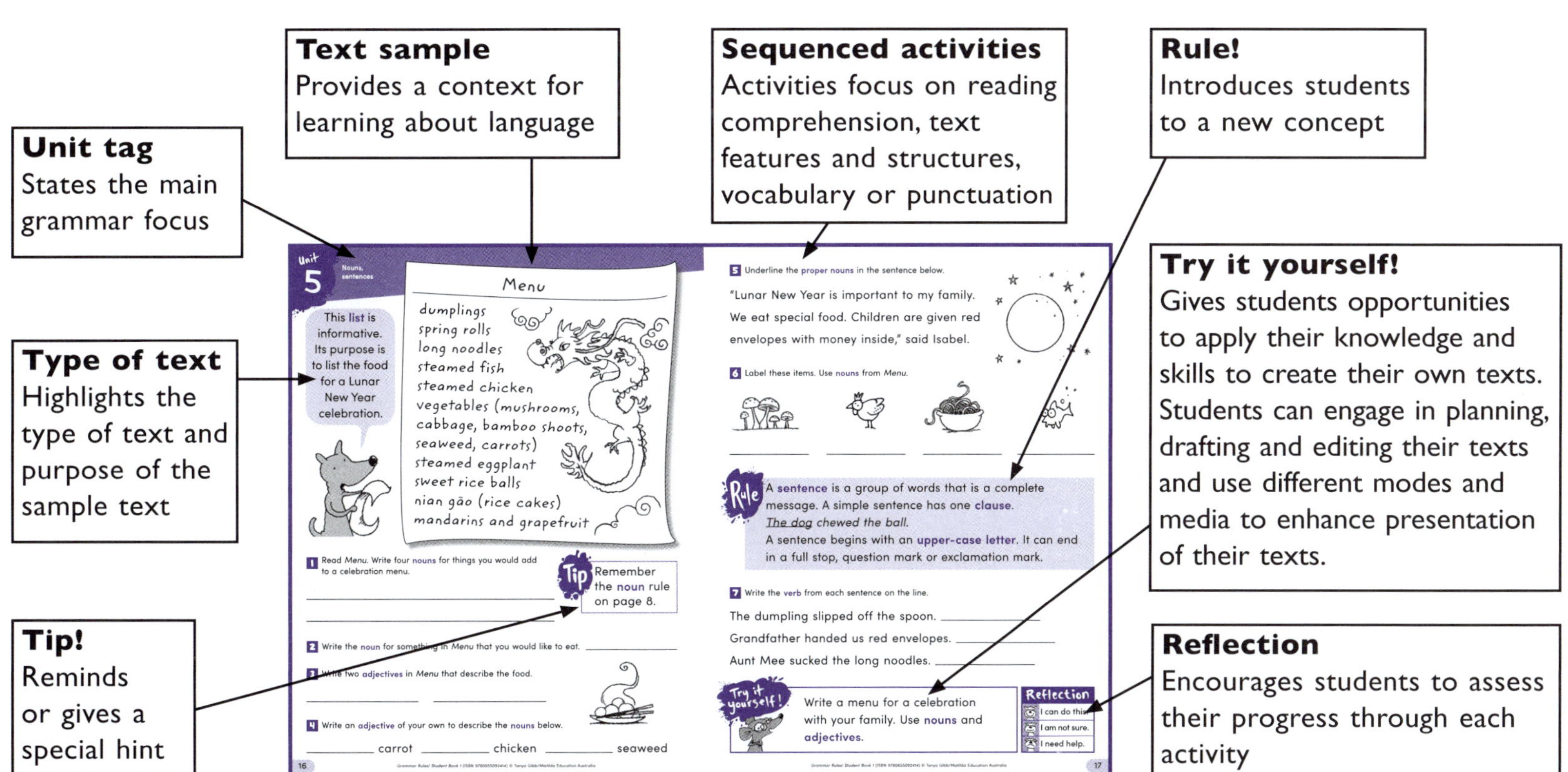

Grammar Rules! Teacher Resource Book 1–2

Full teacher support for *Student Book 1* is provided by *Grammar Rules! Teacher Resource Book 1–2*.

Here you will find valuable background information about teaching English, along with practical resources, such as:

- strategies for teaching text structures and features
- literacy games and activities
- assessment strategies
- teaching tips for every unit in *Student Book 1*
- answers for every unit in *Student Book 1*.

Scope and Sequence

This scope and sequence chart is based on the requirements of the NSW English K–2 Syllabus.

Unit	Unit name/ Type of text	Purpose of text	Clauses, sentences, conjunctions	Nouns, noun groups, pronouns, adjectives	Verbs	Adverbs and prepositional phrases (time and place), time connectives	Elements of language
1	**Things in the Garden** Diagram	to inform	sentences	common nouns	action verbs		labels
2	**A Fish** Diagram	to inform	sentences	common nouns	action verbs	prepositional phrases – place	labels
3	**A Family Tree** Diagram	to inform	sentences	proper nouns, possessive apostrophes			labels
4	**Our Weather Chart** Diagram	to inform	sentences	proper nouns, adjectives	relating verbs		labels
5	**Menu** List	to inform	simple sentences	nouns, adjectives	action verbs		
6	REVISION						
7	**Jobs on the Farm** Map	to inform	commands, sentences	adjectives	action verbs		
8	**At the Playground** Recount	to inform			action verbs	time connectives, prepositional phrases – place	opinions
9	**Class Rules** List	to inform/ instruct	clauses, sentences, commands, exclamations, conjunctions		action verbs		
10	**A Fire Safety Visit** Recount	to inform/ respond	sentences			prepositional phrases – time, time connectives	opinions
11	**Goodbye Elvis** Recount/Reflection	to inform	clauses		saying verbs		opinions
12	REVISION						
13	**A Moreton Bay Fig Tree** Description	to inform	sentences, conjunctions	adjectives			opinions
14	**Jokes**	to entertain	questions, sentences				homophones, word play
15	**Our Favourite Pets** Graph	to inform	clauses, conjunctions, sentences	singular and plural nouns			labels
16	**A Visit from Aunty Violet** Report	to inform/ respond	sentences	adjectives			synonyms, story characters, paragraphs
17	**How to Make an Under the Sea Diorama** Procedure	to inform/ instruct		articles	action verbs		
18	REVISION						

Unit	Unit name/ Type of text	Purpose of text	Clauses, sentences, conjunctions	Nouns, noun groups, pronouns, adjectives	Verbs	Adverbs and prepositional phrases (time and place), time connectives	Elements of language
19	**Sleepy Cat** Poem	to entertain		personal pronouns			rhyme
20	**Dear Uncle Hugh and Uncle Kenan** Personal response	to respond	sentences	personal pronouns, proper nouns, adjectives			opinions and reasons
21	**When I Grow Up** Discussion	to inform/ give an opinion	clauses, conjunctions				opinions and reasons
22	**The Lonely Dragon** Narrative	to entertain	clauses, conjunctions				story characters, setting, plot
23	**How We Get Milk** Explanation	to inform/ explain	sentences				fact and opinion, labels
24	REVISION						
25	**Wednesday and Ruby** Narrative	to entertain	sentences	adjectives	verbs	time connectives	onomatopoeia, story characters, paragraphs
26	**Buy Now!** Advertisement	to persuade			contractions		alliteration, opinion and reason
27	**Sharks** Argument	to persuade	sentences		sensing and thinking verbs		antonyms, opinions and reasons
28	**Cinderfella's Jobs** List	to inform/ instruct	commands			adverbs	
29	**Magic Potion** Recipe	to entertain	commands	noun groups, adjectives	action verbs		
30	REVISION						
31	**Life Cycle** Diagram and Explanation	to inform/ explain	sentences		action verbs		compound words, quotation marks, labels
32	**How to Get Home** Directions and map for imaginary place	to entertain	commands			prepositional phrases	story characters
33	**Book Review** Response	to inform/ respond	sentences, questions	adjectives	verbs		quotation marks, opinion and reason
34	**Koalas** Information report	to inform	clauses, sentences	pronouns, adjectives	relating verbs, saying verbs	prepositional phrases	paragraphs
35	REVISION						

Unit 1

Common nouns, action verbs

This **diagram** is informative. It shows things in a garden.

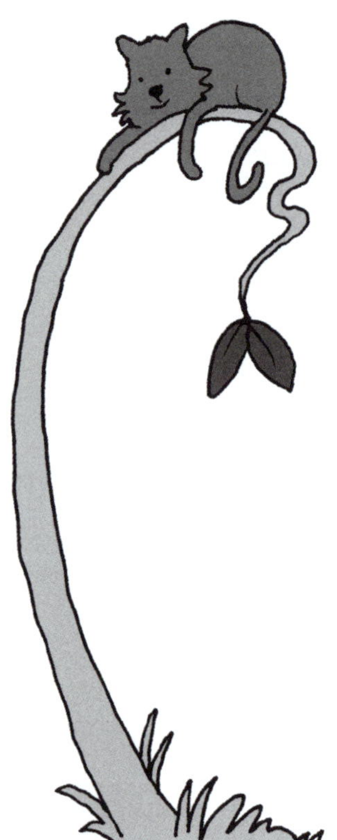

Things in the Garden

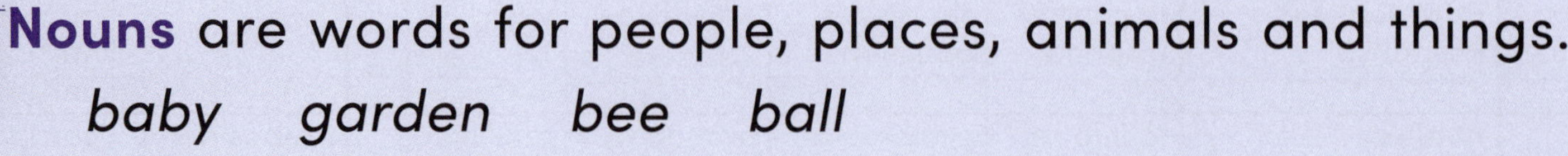

Rule **Nouns** are words for people, places, animals and things.

baby *garden* *bee* *ball*

1 Label the things in the diagram. Write these **nouns** in the boxes.

flower tree bird ball dog

fence bee grass nest frog

Verbs tell what is happening in a sentence.
Action verbs tell the actions.

jump   *is swinging*   *hovered*   *swims*   *splashed*

2 Choose the correct **verbs** from the box to complete the sentences.

hovers
ran
bounced
swims
sits

A bird ______________ in the nest.

A frog ______________ in the pond.

A bee ______________ near the flower.

A ball ______________ on the grass.

My dog ______________ through the garden.

3 Circle the **action verb** in each sentence.

I threw the ball onto the grass. It rolled beside a flower. My dog took it into the pond.

4 Read the story below. Circle the **verb** in each sentence.

The dog played in the garden. A spaceship landed beside her. She ran to it. It flew away.

5 Write a sentence about a real or imaginary garden. Remember to begin your sentence with an **upper-case letter** and end it with a full stop.

____

____

Draw a real or imaginary garden where you would like to play. Label your drawing. Use **nouns**.

This **diagram** is informative. It has labels to give information.

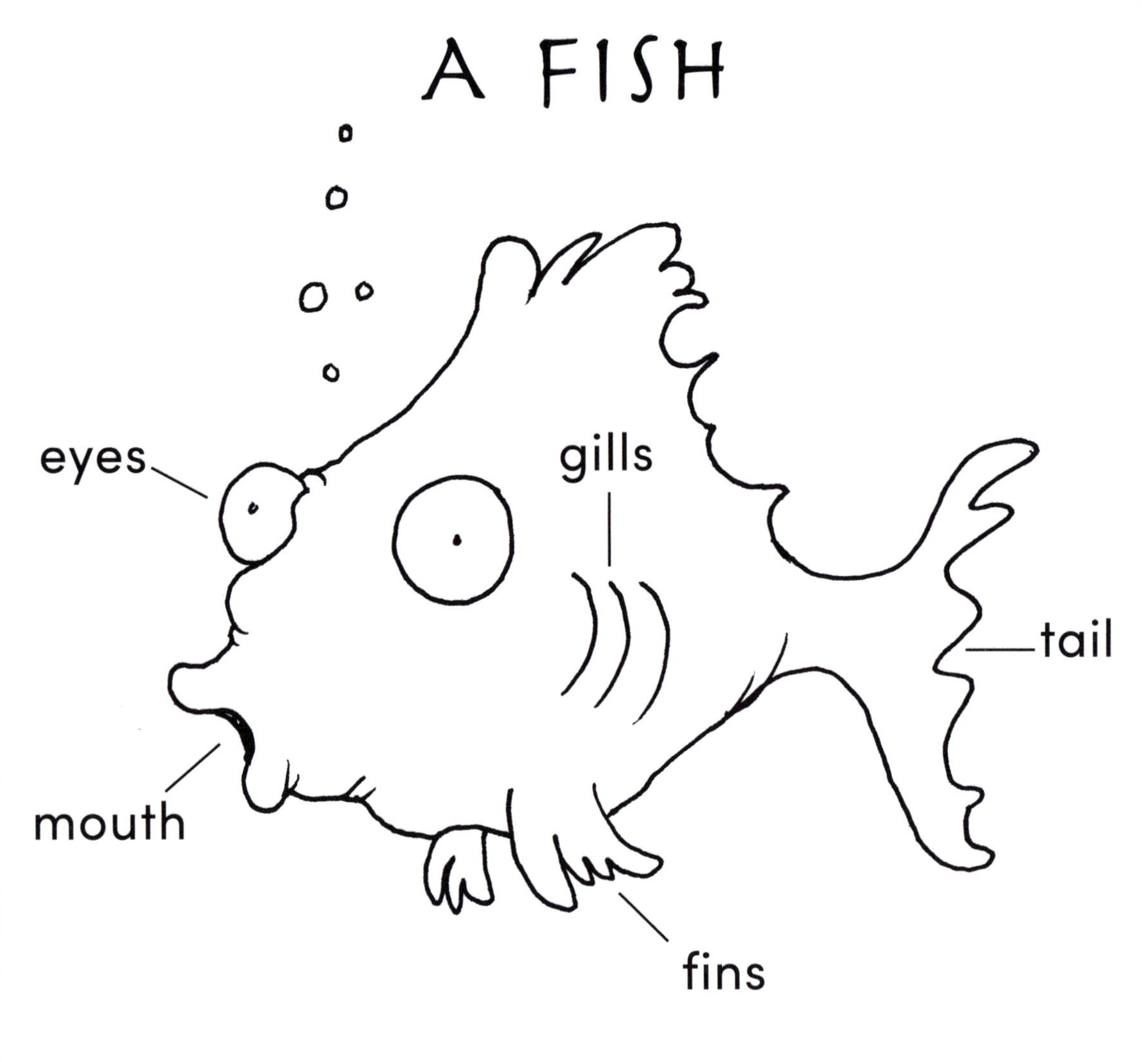

1 Look at the diagram of the fish. Write a **noun** from the diagram on each line.

This is a ____________. It has a ____________.

It has two ____________. It has ____________ and a ____________.

A **prepositional phrase** begins with a **preposition**. It can tell where. *in the ocean* *under a bridge*

2 Choose the correct **prepositional phrase** from the box to complete each simple sentence.

on grasslands	above the water	in the rainforest

Fish leap ____________________.

Zebras gallop ____________________.

Monkeys swing ____________________.

3 Choose a **noun** from the box to label each animal.

dog	duck	koala	sheep

4 Circle the **action verbs** in the sentences below.

The kangaroo bounced across the grass.

It disappeared behind the trees.

Write two **prepositional phrases** from the sentences on the lines.

5 Circle the **action verbs** for things a real-life fish can do.

swim crawl dive float draw eat look breathe

6 Write about an animal and what it does. Use **action verbs**.

Draw a real or imaginary animal. Label your drawing. Use **nouns**.

This **diagram** is informative. The writer's purpose is to show information about family members.

A Family Tree

Grandpa Robert Grandma Claire

Nonno Stefano

Nonna Marie

Stepdad Eddie

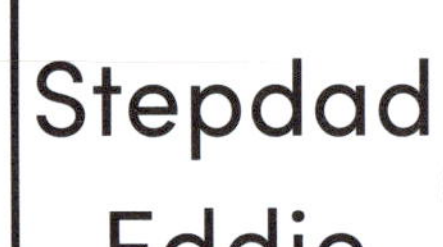

Mum Jilly

Dad Marco

Stepbrother Lachlan

Me Anna

Brother Luca

My cat Tiger

Rule People's names are **proper nouns**.
Proper nouns start with an **upper-case letter**.

1 Look at *A Family Tree*. Write the names of Anna's grandparents.

____________ ____________ ____________ ____________

2 Write a name from *A Family Tree* on each line.

Anna's mum is ____________. Anna's cat is ____________.

Anna's dad is ____________. Anna's brother is ____________.

Grammar Rules! Student Book 1 (ISBN 9780655092414) © Tanya Gibb/Matilda Education Australia

3 Write your name.

Draw a picture of yourself.

4 Write the names of three friends.

5 Write your teacher's name.

Ms Fish

Rule An **apostrophe** can be used to show possession.

Anna's raincoat *Luca's shoes* *the cat's dinner*

6 Rewrite each underlined word correctly with a **possessive apostrophe**.

my friends name ______ Jillys car ______

Robs glasses ______ Lachlans hat ______

7 Write two sentences about your family. Remember to begin your sentence with an **upper-case letter** and end it with a full stop.

Create your own family tree. Use photos or drawings. Label it. Use upper-case letters for **proper nouns**.

Unit 4

Proper nouns, adjectives, relating verbs

This **weather chart** is informative. Its purpose is to give information about the weather.

Monday

Tuesday

Thursday

Friday

hot

windy

cloudy

rainy

cold

foggy

Today is Wednesday

The weather is

We don't come to school on Saturday and Sunday.

Rule The days of the week and the months of the year are **proper nouns**. Proper nouns start with an **upper-case letter**.

March *Saturday* *Monday*

1 Look at *Our Weather Chart*. Write the days of the week in order.

_______________ _______________ _______________ _______________

_______________ _______________ _______________

2 Choose words from *Our Weather Chart* to complete the simple sentences.

Today is _______________.

The weather is _______________.

Adjectives tell more about **nouns**. They can describe.

sunny *happy* *black*

3 Write the seven **adjectives** from *Our Weather Chart*.

__________ __________ __________ __________

__________ __________ __________

Relating verbs tell what things are or have.

It is sunny. *I am hot.* *I have a sun hat.*

4 Circle the **relating verb** in each sentence.

Wednesday was hot.

Today is Friday.

We were busy yesterday.

Sana has a cold.

5 Write an **adjective** from *Our Weather Chart* on each line.

a __________ day

a __________ day

a __________ day

a __________ day

6 Fill in the missing letters. Circle the **nouns** for things you wear on a cold day.

j_mper

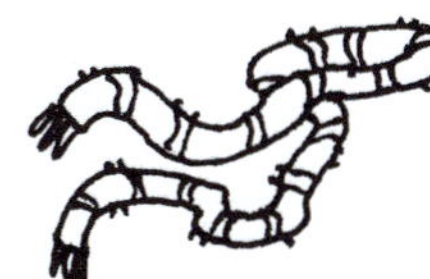

scar_

bean_e

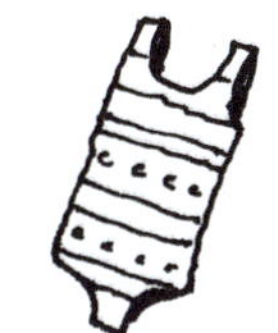

swim__ers

t_ongs

jacke_

short_

Make a poster about weather. Add pictures and words. Tell about the things you can do. Use **adjectives**.

Reflection

 I can do this.

 I am not sure.

 I need help.

This **list** is informative. Its purpose is to list the food for a Lunar New Year celebration.

Menu

dumplings
spring rolls
long noodles
steamed fish
steamed chicken
vegetables (mushrooms, cabbage, bamboo shoots, seaweed, carrots)
steamed eggplant
sweet rice balls
nian gāo (rice cakes)
mandarins and grapefruit

1 Read *Menu*. Write four **nouns** for things you would add to a celebration menu.

____

____

2 Write the **noun** for something in *Menu* that you would like to eat. ____________________

3 Write two **adjectives** in *Menu* that describe the food.

____________________ ____________________

4 Write an **adjective** of your own to describe the **nouns** below.

____________ carrot ____________ chicken ____________ seaweed

Grammar Rules! Student Book 1 (ISBN 9780655092414) © Tanya Gibb/Matilda Education Australia

5 Underline the **proper nouns** in the sentence below.

"Lunar New Year is important to my family. We eat special food. Children are given red envelopes with money inside," said Isabel.

6 Label these items. Use **nouns** from *Menu*.

______________ ______________ ______________ ______________

Rule

A **sentence** is a group of words that is a complete message. A simple sentence has one **clause**.

The dog chewed the ball.

A sentence begins with an **upper-case letter**. It can end in a full stop, question mark or exclamation mark.

7 Write the **verb** from each sentence on the line.

The dumpling slipped off the spoon. ______________

Grandfather handed us red envelopes. ______________

Aunt Mee sucked the long noodles. ______________

Write a menu for a celebration with your family. Use **nouns** and **adjectives**.

Unit 6

Revision

1 Write the **verb** from each sentence on the line.

The sunflower grew towards the sun. ____________________

The tree gave us shelter. ____________________

The frog jumped through the pond. ____________________

Uncle Tomas chopped the eggplant. ____________________

Lunar New Year is a special time. ____________________

The fish has a long tail. ____________________

2 Choose the correct **adjective** from the box. Write it on the line.

happy	sunny	big	pretty

The weather for the picnic is ______________.

A ______________ bird came to our picnic.

We ate our food on a ______________ rug.

Zippy was a ______________ dog at the picnic.

3 Draw a line to link each **noun** to a **proper noun**.

month	Fluffball
day	October
uncle	Abby
aunt	Fred
cat	Wednesday

4 Add **relating verbs** to the sentence.

I __________ six and my brother __________ nine.

5 Write each sentence correctly.

the sheeps name is brittany

____

holly went to nassims home on wednesday

____

6 Circle the **action verbs** in the sentence below.

Maliki bounded across the dirt and disappeared behind the rocks. ("Maliki" is a Warlpiri word for "dog".)

Write two **prepositional phrases** from the sentences on the lines.

____

____

7 Circle the **action verbs** in the sentences below.

A small bird flew over our heads. It landed on the grass.

Write two **prepositional phrases** from the sentences on the lines.

____

____

8 Write a sentence. Describe someone in your family.

____

____

Unit 7

Commands, verbs

This **diagram** is informative. Its purpose is to show where things are on a farm.

Jobs on the Farm

Rule

A **command** is a sentence that tells someone to do something. *Do your homework.*

1 Draw arrows on the diagram above to mark a route around the farm →→→.
Follow these directions.

1. Start at the gate.
2. Feed the pigs.
3. Collect the eggs.
4. Say hello to the cow.
5. Give the dog some water.
6. Hug Mum.
7. Help Dad.

2 Write the **verb** used in each simple sentence on the lines.

The cow stood quietly. ______________

The chicken pecked for breakfast. ______________

A sheep escaped from the paddock. ______________

An apple fell from the tree. ______________

Paolo collected the fallen apples. ______________

Phoebe fed the pigs. ______________

Dad pegged the washing on the line. ______________

3 Write an **adjective** before each noun.

______________ chicken

______________ cow

______________ pig

______________ horse

______________ sheep

4 Draw lines to link each **verb** with the rest of the sentence.

Swim	over the fence.
Jump	an apple.
Eat	across the paddock.
Gallop	some water.
Drink	in the river.

5 What can you do on a farm? Write two sentences.

____

____

Draw a map for your home. Mark a route from your front door to your bed. Write directions to your bed. Begin each **command** with a **verb**.

Unit 8

Action verbs, time connectives

The writer of this text **recounts** events and gives an opinion about the events.

At the Playground

Mira took me to the playground yesterday.

First, we played on the seesaw. Then we went on the slippery dip.

After the slippery dip, Mira pushed me on the swing. She pushed me really high.

Before we went home, we played ball with Mira's dog. We threw the ball for him to chase.

I had great fun at the playground.

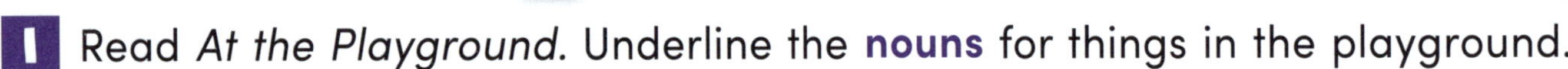

1 Read *At the Playground.* Underline the **nouns** for things in the playground.

2 Find two **prepositional phases** that tell where in *At the Playground.* Write them on the line.

____

3 Choose the correct **action verb** from the box. Write it on the line.

chased	threw	pushed	climbed	went

We ______________ to the playground.

I ______________ the slippery dip ladder.

Mira ______________ the swing.

We ______________ the ball.

Mira's dog ______________ the ball.

Grammar Rules! Student Book 1 (ISBN 9780655092414) © Tanya Gibb/Matilda Education Australia

Time connectives are words that help to sequence events and information in time.

before first second then after next

4 Circle the **time connectives** in *At the Playground.*

5 Write a **time connective** from the box on each line below.

Then
After
First

On Sunday, Jamal and I went to the beach.

______________ we played with a ball on the sand.

______________ we went for a swim. ______________

our swim we built sandcastles.

6 Circle the **verbs** for what a real dog can do.

eat write chase fly read run swim sleep scratch beg

7 Circle **action verbs** that a hand can do.

throw write draw push sit read scratch see fly sneeze

8 Write sentences to tell what each animal is doing.

______________________________ ______________________________

______________________________ ______________________________

Write a **recount** about something you have done. Use **action verbs**. Give your opinion about the activity.

Reflection

 I can do this.

 I am not sure.

 I need help.

Unit 9

Commands, exclamations, conjunctions

These **rules** are informative. Their purpose is to tell children what to do in the classroom.

Class Rules

★ Work quietly.

★ Raise your hand to talk.

★ Listen to others.

★ Look after property.

★ Keep the classroom tidy.

★ Walk inside.

★ ______________________________

★ ______________________________

1 Read *Class Rules*. Each rule is a **command**. Underline the **action verbs**.

2 Write two extra **commands** at the end of *Class Rules*.

3 Write a **command** that a family member gives you.

____

Remember the **command** rule on page 20.

4 Write a **command** in each speech bubble.

Rule

A **conjunction** (*and, but, or, so*) can join simple sentences to make a **compound sentence**.

Raise your hand to talk. Listen to others.

Raise your hand to talk and listen to others.

5 Underline the **conjunction** in this sentence.

Buy a fire extinguisher and learn how to use it.

6 Write a rule for your kitchen at home. Use a **conjunction** to write a compound sentence.

____

Some commands are **exclamations**. Exclamations are spoken loudly or in anger or surprise. They end in an **exclamation mark**.

Stop! *Look!* *No!*

★Have more fun!

7 Write an **exclamation** from the box on each line to show what you would shout at each event.

Stop!	Run!	Help!

A toddler is about to run onto the road. ____________

You are going to fall out of a tree. ____________

Your sister is playing soccer. ____________

Write a set of **rules** for safety in the water or safety with an animal.

Reflection

- I can do this.
- I am not sure.
- I need help.

Unit 10

Prepositional phrases, time connectives

A Fire Safety Visit

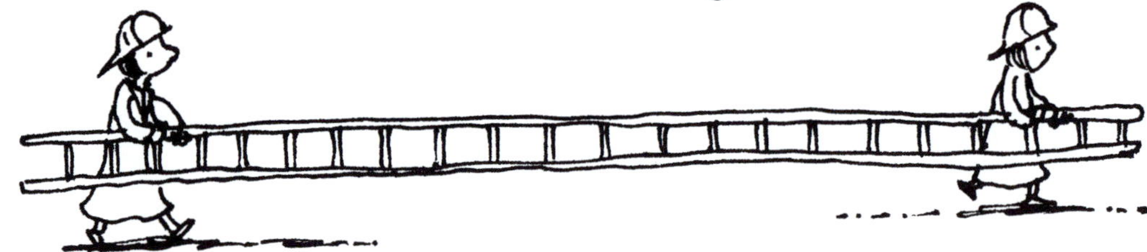

Firefighters visited our school today. First, they talked to us about fire safety in our homes. They said we all needed fire escape plans. Fire escape plans let everyone know what to do if there is a fire. Next, they told us about smoke alarms. Then we took turns to sit in the fire engine. It was very exciting.

1 Read *A Fire Safety Visit*. Underline the **time connectives**.

2 Draw a line to match each person to their role.

Tip Remember the **time connectives** rule on page 23.

A firefighter	looks after your teeth.
A dentist	gives their time to help others.
An ambulance officer	helps to keep you safe.
A police officer	teaches you things.
An elder	cares for animals.
A vet	helps if you are hurt or sick.
A volunteer	puts out fires.

Grammar Rules! Student Book 1 (ISBN 9780655092414) © Tanya Gibb/Matilda Education Australia

Rule **Prepositional phrases** can help to sequence events in time. These phrases tell <u>when</u>.

in the morning *after dinner* *before lunch*

3 Write numbers 1 to 5 in the boxes to show the sequence in time.

☐ in the morning	☐ during lunch	☐ at bedtime
☐ after lunch	☐ before dinner	

4 Choose the correct phrases from the box to tell <u>when</u>. Write the phrases on the lines.

at night
in the morning
at sunset
at sunrise
in the afternoon

I eat breakfast ____________________.

I go to bed ____________________.

I get home from school ____________________.

The sun goes down ____________________.

The sun comes up ____________________.

5 Write a sentence for each **noun** below. Remember to use correct punctuation.

nurse	dentist	vet	coach

____

____

____

____

Write a **recount** about an event at school. Use **time connectives**.

Reflection

- I can do this.
- I am not sure.
- I need help.

Unit 11

Saying verbs, clauses

Goodbye Elvis

My pet mouse became very sick on Friday. He did not move. He did not eat. He was very skinny and he had dull fur.

Mum and I took him to the vet. The vet told me that my mouse was dying. I did not want my mouse to suffer so I asked the vet to put him to sleep. I held him and the vet gave him a needle. He went to sleep and died very quickly. It was very sad and I cried.

This **recount** is informative. The writer's purpose is to retell events and express their feelings.

1 Read *Goodbye Elvis*. Write the **prepositional phrase** in the text that tells when the mouse became sick.

____

2 How does the writer of *Goodbye Elvis* feel? ______________

3 Circle the **verbs** in these simple sentences.

My pet mouse became very sick on Friday.

Mum and I took him to the vet.

Rule

Saying verbs tell that something is being said or has been said.

asked *told* *cried* *shouted* *said*

4 Circle the two **saying verbs** in *Goodbye Elvis*.

5 Choose the correct **saying verb** from the box. Write it on the line.

gurgled whispered told asked giggled

Lauren ________________ at the clown.

Mum ________________ me to be quiet.

Dad ________________ for my help.

Nia ________________ in her stroller.

Chandra ________________ me a secret.

6 *"I love you," said Mum.* Circle **saying verbs** you could use instead of *said.*

whispered chuckled giggled

barked **said** cried

yelled meowed

announced

7 Draw a line to link each **saying verb** to an animal.

cheeped	chicken
clucked	horse
mooed	donkey
neighed	cow
brayed	bird

8 Write a **saying verb** from the box for each animal.

woofed	quacked
growled	snorted

The duck ________________.

The dog ________________.

The pig ________________.

The possum ________________.

Write a **recount**. Include things people have said. Use **saying verbs.**

Grammar Rules! Student Book 1 (ISBN 9780655092414) © Tanya Gibb/Matilda Education Australia

Unit 12 Revision

1 In each speech bubble, write a **command** for the dog.

2 Write a **prepositional phrase** that tells <u>when</u> on each line.

"Can I do my homework ______

____________?" asked Riku.

"I want to watch TV __________

__________," announced Daniil.

3 Draw a line to link each **noun** to an **action verb**.

A shark	flies.
A kangaroo	swims.
A monkey	jumps.
A snake	swings.
A bird	slithers.

4 Circle the **conjunction** that joins the clauses in each sentence.

Cut the cake but don't eat the cake yet.

Wash the dog and she can dry off outside.

It's going to rain so take an umbrella.

5 Join the two sentences with a **conjunction**. Rewrite them as one sentence.

I think I will buy a book. I might buy a ball.

____

____

6 Write numbers 1 to 5 in the boxes to <u>sequence</u> the events in time.

- [ ] After breakfast I cleaned my teeth.
- [ ] This morning I woke at 7 o'clock.
- [ ] Then I had breakfast.
- [ ] After that I got dressed.
- [ ] Then I came to school.

7 Circle the **verb** in each sentence.

My cat sleeps all day.

Alejandro ate a pie.

A kangaroo jumped past.

Misty chewed a shoe.

The storm knocked down the tree.

8 Write an **exclamation** from the box in each speech bubble.

Wow!	NO!	Hurrah!

9 Choose the correct **saying verb** from the box. Write it on the line.

ordered	asked	croaked	howled	laughed

"That was funny," ________________ Dad.

"Do you think so?" ________________ Mum.

"Ribbipp," ________________ the frog.

"Wooosh!" ________________ the wind.

"Clean your teeth," ________________ the dentist.

Unit 13

Sentences, conjunctions

A Moreton Bay Fig Tree

The writer's purpose is to describe the Moreton Bay fig tree and give an opinion about it.

The tree in our school playground is a Moreton Bay fig tree. It has a thick trunk and thick branches. I love the way its twisty roots stick up above the ground. It's really old. My teacher thinks it is at least one hundred years old. It gives birds and insects a place to live. It gives us shade all year round. I eat my lunch under its canopy every day. It's a beautiful tree.

1 Read *A Moreton Bay Fig Tree*. Write three reasons the writer likes the Moreton Bay fig tree.

2 Join the simple sentences. Use a **conjunction** to make a compound sentence. Write it on the line.

The tree is really big. I sit in its shade.

____

3 Draw a line to link the parts of the **sentences**.

Ben ate	the road.
Min held	the car.
Jamal washed	my hand.
Ling crossed	two bananas.

4 Unjumble the **sentences**. Rewrite them correctly. Use **upper-case letters** and full stops.

dad pancakes cooked

____

brother my haircut got a

____

the silly was clown

____

seagulls the dog chased

____

5 Add **full stops** where they are needed.

The tree is tall It has strong branches It is a gum tree

6 Draw a line to link the parts of each **command**.

Sit	your lunch.
Eat	away your lunch box.
Throw	under the tree.
Pack	your rubbish in the bin.

Remember the **command** rule on page 20.

7 Write a **command** to give your classmates.

____

Write a **description** of something at your school. Use **upper-case letters** and full stops in all your **sentences**.

These jokes are imaginative. Their purpose is to entertain through word play.

Jokes

1. Question: What do moths study in school?
   Answer: Mothematics.

2. Question: Why is six afraid of seven?
   Answer: Because seven eight nine.

3. Knock Knock.
   Who's there?
   Boo.
   Boo who?
   Don't cry, it's only a joke.

Rule A **question** is a sentence that asks something. It ends in a **question mark**.

Are you hungry?

1 Read the jokes to a friend. Underline the **question** in each joke.

2 Write a silly **question** you might ask a teacher.

___

Write a silly **question** you might ask a parent.

___

Where are you going?

A **homophone** is a word that sounds the same as another word but has a different meaning.

bear bare *pear pair pare* *to too two*

3 What is the homophone in *Jokes*? ______________________________

4 Write silly **questions** these people might ask.

5 Add a **question mark** or a **full stop** at the end of each sentence.

I love pigs ☐

Where do you live ☐

Do pigs fly ☐

I live in Wellington ☐

Work with a group of friends. Collect riddles and other jokes with **questions**. Make a book of jokes.

Reflection

I can do this.

I am not sure.

I need help.

Unit 15 Singular and plural nouns, clauses, conjunctions

This **graph** is informative. Its purpose is to show the results of a vote.

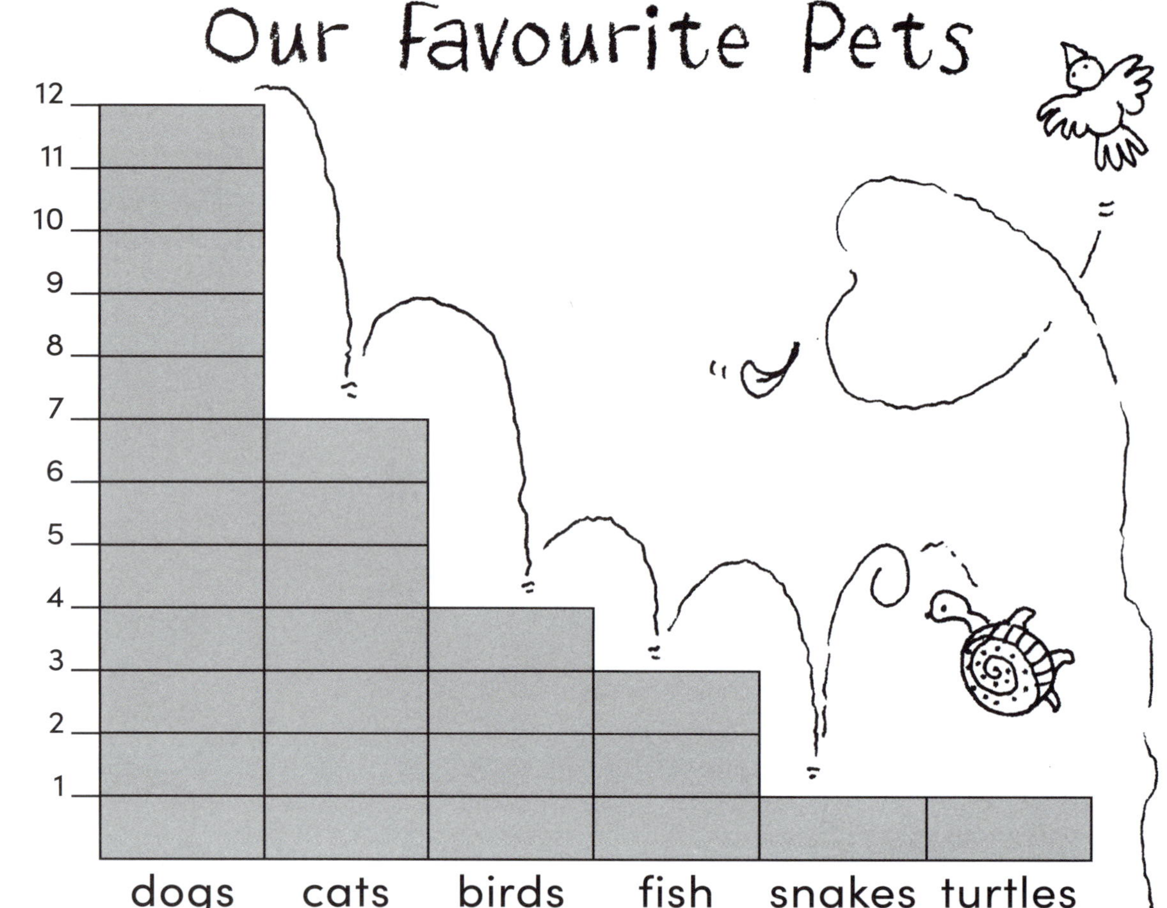

Our class voted on our favourite pets.
Twelve people think that dogs are the best pets.
Seven people think cats are best.
Four people like birds best.
Three people like fish best.
One person prefers snakes and one person prefers turtles.
So, dogs are the most popular pets for people in our class.

A **singular noun** names one person, place, animal or thing.
A **plural noun** names more than one. *hat* → *hats*

1 Read *Our Favourite Pets*. Now add ***s*** to make the **plural** for each **noun**.

one dog → two dogs

one cat → three __________

one bird → four __________

one snake → some __________

one girl → many __________

one boy → lots of __________

2 Add ***es*** to make the **plural** for each **noun**.

one sandwich → two sandwiches one dress → three ________

one peach → four ________ one box → some ________

3 Write the **plural** for each **noun**.

one person → many people one fish → lots of ________

one child → some ________ a fly → many ________

one loaf of bread → two ________ of bread

one tooth → all the ________

4 Label the pictures. Write a number and a **plural noun** or **singular noun**.

two pigs ________ ________ ________

5 Read *Our Favourite Pets*. Find the sentence that has two clauses joined by a **conjunction**. Write it on the lines.

____

____

6 What is your favourite kind of pet? ________________________

7 Finish the sentence.

If I had a pet dragon, I ________________________

____

Ask your classmates to vote for their favourite pets. Make a **graph** to show how they voted.

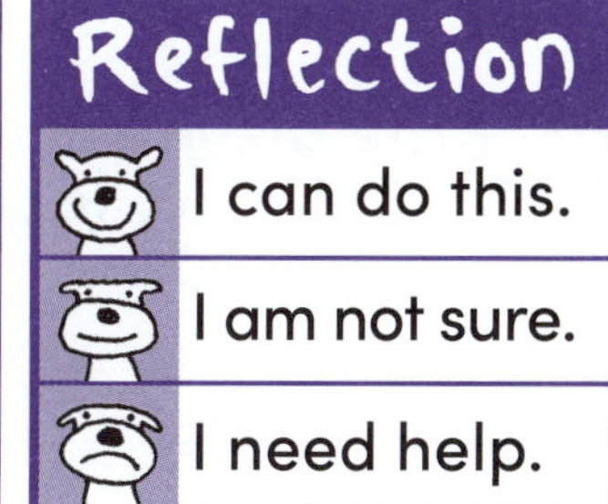

Unit 16

Adjectives, synonyms, story characters

This is a **report**. The writer's purpose is to report to readers about a visitor to the school.

A Visit from Aunty Violet

We had an interesting visitor at school today. Her name was Aunty Violet.

Aunty Violet told us Dreaming stories and about her clan, the Gadigal people. Our school is on Gadigal country. Aunty Violet said that her ancestors had lived here for thousands of years before Captain Cook came here from England.

Aunty Violet is a good storyteller.

By Oliver

1 Read *A Visit from Aunty Violet.* Underline the **proper nouns**.

2 Find two **adjectives** in the text. Write them on the lines.

____

____

Tip Remember the **adjective** rule on page 15.

3 Circle the **verb** in each sentence.

"Budyeri kamaru," said Aunty Violet. "'Budyeri kamaru' is 'hello' in the Gadigal language."

4 Write a sentence from *A Visit from Aunty Violet* that lets you know that Oliver was happy about Aunty Violet's visit.

____

Rule

Characters in stories are described in specific ways to influence the way the reader feels about them.
Ethelred was always cranky. Bertram was sweet and kind.

5 Circle the **adjectives** below that would help to make the monster a likeable story character.

soft handsome cute
angry sweet
ugly kind
nasty funny
happy beautiful

6 In stories, there are many types of characters. Draw a line to link each **adjective** to a **noun** for a possible story character.

fierce	villain
brave	giraffe
curious	lion
sneaky	hero
evil	rat

7 Write as many **adjectives** as you can to describe a type of story character that you would NOT like.

Rule

Synonyms are words that have similar meanings.
big → enormous

8 Circle all the words that mean *small*.

tiny enormous little
great incy wincy
minuscule petite big

9 Circle the **synonym** for "tribe" used in *A Visit from Aunty Violet*.

gathering club clan
country friends

Write a **description** of an animal character for a story. Use **adjectives**.

Reflection

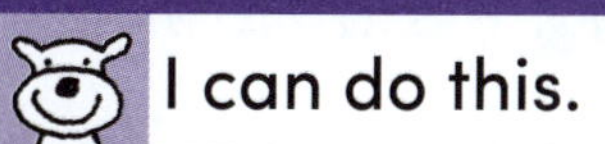 I can do this.

 I am not sure.

 I need help.

This text is informative. Its purpose is to instruct how to make a diorama.

HOW TO MAKE AN UNDER THE SEA DIORAMA

What you need:

box
blue paint
felt-tip pens
scissors
coloured paper
cotton thread
tape
glue
rocks or pebbles

What to do:

1. Paint the inside of the box blue for the water.
2. Colour and cut out paper fish shapes.
3. Hang the fish inside the box on cotton thread.
4. Make coloured paper plants and reeds.
5. Place pebbles or rocks on the bottom of the box.

Instructions usually list equipment needed and what you have to do.

1 Read *How to Make an Under the Sea Diorama.* Circle the **action verb** in each instruction.

2 Write five **nouns** used in *How to Make an Under the Sea Diorama.*

Grammar Rules!

______________________'s Writing Log

1 Think! Make a plan

What is your topic?
What is the purpose of the text?
Who is the audience?
What type of text and text form will you use?
Will a graphic organiser help?

2 Draft

Gather your ideas.
Have a go at writing.

3 Revise

Reread your writing.
Read your writing to a partner.
Read your writing to your teacher.
Ask for help to improve meaning.

4 Proofread

Check your grammar.
Check your spelling.
Check your punctuation.

5 Publish

Publish and share your text.
Reflect on your work.

Each time you finish a piece of writing, record it in the log. Give it a rating.

Rating scale

A good start.

Doing well.

Brilliant!

Date	Write the title of your text.	Text purpose, mode and medium	Audience
Write the date.	Write the title of your piece.	eg recount/email	Who were you writing for or to

Do you need some ideas for other text forms to try? Look at the back page!

Grammar I used	My rating	Where to next?
.ist the main grammar features you used.	Record your rating.	What would you like to try next? Does your teacher have any comments?

I've tried these types of texts and text forms . . .

Narrative (imaginative)

- [ ] Story
- [ ] Comic
- [ ] Other ________________

Recount

(imaginative or informative)

- [ ] Letter
- [ ] Other ________________

Description

(imaginative or informative)

- [ ] Poem
- [ ] Letter
- [ ] Other ________________

Information report

(informative)

- [ ] Website
- [ ] Other ________________

Procedure (informative)

- [ ] Cookbook
- [ ] Game rules
- [ ] Other ________________

Explanation (informative)

- [ ] Reference book
- [ ] Other ________________

Persuasion (persuasive)

(argues one side of an issue)

- [ ] Speech
- [ ] TV advertisement
- [ ] Poster
- [ ] Other ________________

Discussion (informative/persuasive/reflective) (presents a number of viewpoints)

- [ ] Conversation
- [ ] Other ________________

Response

(informative/persuasive)

- [ ] Diary
- [ ] Book review
- [ ] Poem
- [ ] Other ________________

3 Draw lines to link the parts of each **command**.

Share	the ice-cream.
Peel	the chocolates.
Pour	the potatoes.
Lick	the watermelon.
Cut	the milk.

4 Complete each **command** for a dog. Use an **action verb** from the box.

Roll	Run	Jump	Chase	Lie

__________ down.

__________ the ball.

__________ through the hoop.

__________ over.

__________ around the park.

Rule

Articles are *a, an, the*. Use *a* for words beginning with a consonant. Use *an* for words beginning with a vowel. Use *the* for a specific noun. *a box* *an eel* *the shark*

5 Write the correct **article** (*a, an, the*) on each line.

I cut _______ red fish carefully for my diorama.

I will make _______ wild animal diorama next week.

My next diorama will have _______ lion and _______ elephant.

6 Tick each sentence that is a **command**.

I love guinea pigs. ☐

Can you count to 100? ☐

Kiss me. ☐

Finish your dinner. ☐

Get a haircut. ☐

Where's Mum? ☐

Try it yourself!

Write a set of **instructions** for making something. Start each instruction with an **action verb**.

Reflection

I can do this.

I am not sure.

I need help.

Unit 18
Revision

1 Write a **sentence** to answer each **question**.

What did you have for breakfast?

____

What is your favourite food?

____

2 Add a **full stop**, an **exclamation mark** or a **question mark** to the end of each sentence.

The gorilla would like some fruit ☐

Please feed the gorilla ☐

Look out for the spider ☐

Can you grow a moustache ☐

I cannot grow a moustache ☐

3 Write the correct **article** on each line.

Rover, ________ dog, barks a lot.

Pass me ________ piece of cake with the strawberry on it.

I'll buy ________ banana from the tuck shop.

Charlotte wants ________ apple.

4 Write the **plural** for each **noun**.

one egg → two ____________

one tooth → three ____________

one flower → two ____________

one child → many ____________

5 Follow the string to see what each animal is doing. Write the **sentences** on the lines.

The lion	is sleeping.	______________________
The bear	is eating.	______________________
The possum	is swimming.	______________________
The rat	is prowling.	______________________
The shark	is sneaking.	______________________

6 Write a **question** in each speech bubble.

It's 2 o'clock.

I forgot to bring it.

7 *Mum was <u>angry</u> when I lost my school jumper.* Circle **synonyms** for *angry*.

peaceful furious happy mad cranky

pleased confused sad excited

8 Circle the **adjectives** that could describe a duck that is a story character.

quacked sky yellow sun

fluffy flower fly flew

bug lost angry talkative

Sleepy Cat

Cleopatra is
a tabby cat.
We got her
at the pound.
She loves to sleep
on Daddy's lap.
Her tummy's
very round.

She sleeps
on brick walls
in the sun.
She sleeps
on Mummy's chair.
She sleeps and eats
and sleeps and purrs
and sleeps
just everywhere.

Rule

Personal pronouns can be used in place of nouns.

me I we us you he him she her it they them

Ella and William are at the park. They will be home soon.

1 Read *Sleepy Cat*. Which two **pronouns** are used for Cleopatra? Underline them in the poem.

______________________ ______________________

2 Find the **personal pronoun** "We" in *Sleepy Cat*. Who does "We" mean?

____

3 What is a *pound* in the poem?

____

4 How does the poet want you to feel about Cleopatra? Write a sentence to answer.

____

5 Choose the correct **personal pronoun** from the box. Write it on the line. If it begins a sentence use an **upper-case letter**.

she
I
her
they
he

________ are coming to the concert.

Robert is missing. Where is ________?

Uncle Vince and ________ like lasagne.

________ threw her shoe on the roof.

I like ________.

6 Write a **personal pronoun** on each line.

Bilal and Sienna went to the shop.

__________ bought bananas.

Bilal is going to make a banana cake.

__________ will take an hour to cook.

Rule **Rhyming** words have the same <u>end</u> sound.

hair pear bare where

7 Find and write the two pairs of rhyming words in the poem.

______________ ______________

______________ ______________

8 Write six rhyming words for *chair.*

____

Write a poem about an animal. Use **pronouns** in the place of nouns when it makes sense.

Reflection

- I can do this.
- I am not sure.
- I need help.

Unit 20 Proper nouns

This is a letter. The writer's purpose is to **respond** to a holiday event.

Dear Uncle Hugh and Uncle Kenan,

I had a good time at your house during the holidays. Thank you for taking me to the aquarium. I liked the octopus, the sea star, the stingray and the shark. The most interesting thing at the aquarium was the shark egg. I didn't know that shark eggs looked like big plastic corkscrews.

Love Lana

Mr Hugh Doyle and Mr Kenan Ceric
2 Hastings Road
North Ryde
NSW

Names for particular places are **proper nouns**.
Proper nouns start with an **upper-case letter**.

Australia *Canberra* *New Zealand*

1 Read *Dear Uncle Hugh and Uncle Kenan*. Underline three **proper nouns** for people's names.

2 Write the **proper noun** place names from the address on the envelope.

___

3 Write the **proper nouns** for your school's name.

___

4 Write the **proper noun** or **proper nouns** for your town or suburb.

____

5 Rewrite the **proper nouns** correctly. Start each one with an **upper-case letter**.

australia ______________ mongo street ______________________

pookipoo public school ______________________________________

aunty tilly __________________ uncle bing ___________________

crazy kids child care centre _________________________________

new zealand ______________________

6 Write your address on the envelope.

____

____

____

____

7 What did Lana say shark eggs look like?

____

____

8 Write three **adjectives** from Lana's letter to Uncle Hugh and Uncle Kenan.

____

____

____

9 Colour the things you might find at an aquarium.

elephant sea star octopus sea jelly koala stingray shark sheep

Try it yourself!

Write a **response** to something you have seen or a place you have been. Give your opinion about it.

Reflection

I can do this.

I am not sure.

I need help.

When I Grow Up

Some people in my class want to be pop stars when they grow up because they want to be rich and famous.

Other people in my class want to be police officers or firefighters because they want to help people and have adventures.

I want to be a teacher when I grow up because I want to be the boss and I like helping little children.

The writer's purpose is to present different opinions about jobs and their own opinion.

1 Read *When I Grow Up*. Circle the **personal pronouns**.

Remember the **personal pronoun** rule on page 44.

2 Circle the **sentences**.

Where jump
go shop glue
television shows
Sunglasses
I will buy a sandwich.
Follow the path.
chicken and mince
spaghetti bolognaise
Laura has a new watch.

Rule

Conjunctions (*but, because, although, unless, so, and, but, or*) can link clauses when giving opinions.

I love dolphins <u>because</u> they are very smart <u>and</u> they love their families.

3 Underline the **conjunctions** in *When I Grow Up*.

4 Draw lines to link each opinion with a reason.

I hate washing our dog	because my friends are there.
I like choir practice	but only when it's very ripe.
I love pineapple	because she shakes water all over me.

5 Write a **conjunction** from the box to join the clauses.

so	and	but	or	because

Georgia wants to be a chef ____________ she loves cooking.

Nico hopes to be athlete ____________ he'd better get fit.

Leo wants to be a circus clown ____________ he doesn't like face paint.

Hugo can skate ____________ Mulan can skate too.

Isla might be a truck driver ____________ she might join the army.

6 What would you like to be when you grow up? Finish the sentence.

When I grow up I would like to be ______________________

because ______________________________.

7 Write your **opinions**.

My favourite television show is ______________________

because ______________________________

____

My favourite book is ______________________

because ______________________________

____

Ask classmates what they want to be when they grow up. Write a **discussion** that gives their **opinions**.

Unit 22

Clauses, conjunctions

This **narrative** is about an imaginary character. The narrative has a beginning, a middle and an end.

The Lonely Dragon

Once upon a time, on top of a mountain, in a land far, far away, there lived a dragon. She lived all alone because a knight had killed her parents. The dragon was sad and very lonely. She wanted a friend.

The dragon decided to leave her home and fly to the far corners of the earth to search for other dragons. She had many adventures but after a long, long time she finally found another sad and very lonely dragon. She was so excited.

The dragons flew together to her mountain-top home and they lived happily ever after.

1 When and where does the story begin?

____

2 How did the dragon feel at the beginning of the story? ______________________

3 What did the dragon want? ______________________

4 Complete this sentence.

At the end of the story, the dragon felt ______________________

because ______________________.

5 Choose the correct **conjunctions** from the box to join the clauses.

and so because but

The dragon left home __________ she was lonely.

The dragon has a tail ________ she also has wings.

The dragon flew around the world ______ she could find a friend.

The dragon was friendly ________ she didn't have any friends.

6 Choose the best ending for each sentence. Write it on the line.

all the way to China.	happily ever after.
to the mountain top.	a friend.

The dragon flew ______________________________

In China the dragon found ______________________________

Together the two dragons flew ______________________________

They lived ______________________________

7 Choose the correct **conjunctions** to join the clauses.

and so because but

I like snails __________ I don't like slugs.

I like snails __________ they leave a trail.

I eat crusts __________ my hair will go curly.

The dog ate a snail __________ it also ate a slug.

Write an adventure story about imaginary characters. Make sure it has a beginning, a middle and an end.

Reflection

- I can do this.
- I am not sure.
- I need help.

This informative text is an **explanation** in the form of a flow diagram. It shows how we get milk.

How We Get Milk

Machines pump milk from the cow's udder.

Refrigerated trucks take the milk to the factory.

The milk is heated to kill any germs.

Then it is cooled again.

The milk is put in cartons and bottles.

Refrigerated trucks take the cartons and bottles to shops.

1 Read *How We Get Milk*. Now write numbers 1 to 6 in the boxes to show the sequence.

- ☐ The milk is cooled.
- ☐ The milk is bottled.
- ☐ The milk is heated.
- ☐ The milk goes to the factory.
- ☐ The milk goes to the shop.
- ☐ The milk is pumped out of the cow.

Grammar Rules! Student Book 1 (ISBN 9780655092414) © Tanya Gibb/Matilda Education Australia

Tip A **sentence** can be a **fact**. *My teacher is Mr Smart.*
A **sentence** can give an **opinion**. *Mr Smart is fabulous.*

2 Write *fact* or *opinion* after each **sentence**.

Cows have udders. ________ I like oat milk best. ________

Cows make milk. ________ Cows have four legs. ________

Cows are cute. ________ Baby cows drink milk. ________

3 The sentences are muddled. Write them correctly. Use **upper-case letters** and full stops.

females are cows ________

are males bulls ________

calves baby cows called are ________

udders suck milk from calves ________

4 Write a word from the box on each line.

they	milked	drink	milk

Cows are usually ________ twice a day. On some farms ________ are milked three times a day. Cows need to ________ a lot of water to make ________.

5 Write **rhyming** words.

cow ________ ________

day ________ ________

Work with a partner or in a group. Find out how we get a different food. Draw a flow diagram to explain the <u>sequence</u>. Label the diagram with facts.

Reflection

- I can do this.
- I am not sure.
- I need help.

Grammar Rules! Student Book 1 (ISBN 9780655092414) © Tanya Gibb/Matilda Education Australia

Unit 24

Revision

1 Write **rhyming** words.

sad ____________ ____________ sleep ____________ ____________

tent ____________ ____________ round ____________ ____________

2 Write the numbers 1 to 4 to show the sequence.

Watch the plant grow.	Plant a seed.	Water the seed.	Watch the flower grow.
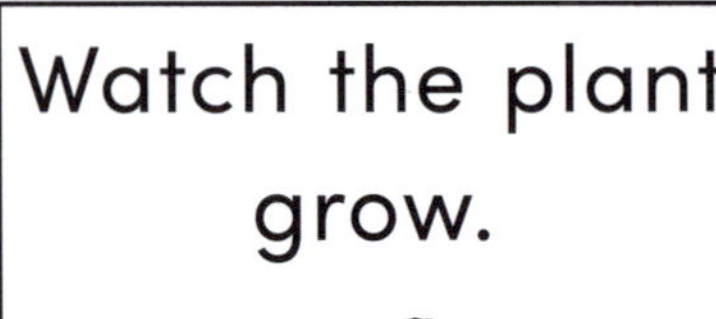			
☐	☐	☐	☐

3 Circle the words that let you know the pigs are happy.

Polly and Peter were excited to be outside in the sunshine. They loved Scarlet.

How else can you tell the pigs are happy?

____

4 Choose the correct **personal pronoun** from the box. Write it on the line.

you they he she

Are Ted and Jenny coming? Yes __________ are.

Will Nazeem come too? Yes __________ will.

Will Leilani come too? Yes __________ will.

Can I come? Yes __________ can.

5 Circle the **personal pronouns**.

go said you us me he she it

shop them they yell sink house

Grammar Rules! Student Book 1 (ISBN 9780655092414) © Tanya Gibb/Matilda Education Australia

6 Rewrite each **sentence** correctly. Use **upper-case letters** and full stops.

yasmin lives in naarm, which is melbourne

____

eddie lives on baker street in mildura

____

aunty maggie lives in dunedoo

____

7 Write *fact* or *opinion* after each sentence.

Iceblocks are yummier than ice-creams. ______________

Magpies can fly. ______________ Emus can't fly. ______________

Dogs have ears. ______________ I love rainy days. ______________

8 Write a **fact** about something. ______________________________

____

Write an **opinion** about something. Give a reason for your opinion. ______________

____

9 Use a **conjunction** from the box in each sentence to join the clauses.

and	so	but	because

I love Nan ______________ I love Pa.

I have ten fingers ______________ I only have two hands.

I brought my raincoat ______________ Mum thinks it's going to rain.

I brought my ball ______________ we can play soccer.

This imaginative text is part of a **narrative**. It introduces the main character and the character's problem.

Wednesday and Ruby

Once upon a time there was a puppy called Wednesday. She had a basket to sleep in, her own bowl to drink from, toys to play with and a human family to love her.

One day there was a huge storm. The wind howled. The rain thundered. The trees swished and swooshed. The branches smashed and crashed. Wednesday was scared.

Wednesday ran to get away from the storm. She ran and ran and by the time the storm was over she was lost. She began to cry. A sheep heard her cries.

The sheep said, "My name is Ruby. Don't cry. I will help you."

1 Read *Wednesday and Ruby*. The main character is ____________________.

2 Circle the **adjectives** that describe the puppy's home.

scary loving happy cold wet

uncomfortable comfortable loud

3 Why did the puppy cry?

____

4 Add **verbs** from the story *Wednesday and Ruby* to complete the sentences.

The wind ______________.

The rain ______________.

The trees ______________ and ______________.

The branches ______________ and ______________.

5 Draw a line to match the food with the **prepositional phrase** that tells when you are most likely to eat it.

I have a sandwich and an apple	in the morning.
I have a banana on toast	at lunchtime.
I have noodles and vegetables	at dinnertime.

Rule **Onomatopoeia** is when words sound like the thing they represent. *creak* *plop* *slurp*

creak

6 Find four **onomatopoeia** words in *Wednesday and Ruby*.

______________ ______________ ______________ ______________

7 Write the correct **onomatopoeia** words on the lines.

Splat!	Snuffle thud!	Boom!	Chug chug chug!

__________! went the raindrops. __________! went the thunder.

__________ __________! went the possum in the roof.

__________ __________ __________! went the old steam train.

Try it yourself! Write an ending for *Wednesday and Ruby*. Does the puppy get home? Make sure to tell how the characters feel.

Reflection

- I can do this.
- I am not sure.
- I need help.

This persuasive text is an advertisement. Its purpose is to persuade people to buy something.

1 Read *Buy Now!* What is the name of the drink in the advertisement?

____

2 Write the **adjective** in *Buy Now!* that says what colour the drink is. ______________

Write the **adjective** that says what the drink tastes like. ______________

3 Do you think you would like to try this drink? ______________

What might make someone want to try it?

____

What might make someone not want to try it?

____

Is *Buy Now!* selling to children or adults? ______________

Rule

Alliteration is when the beginning of words sound the same.

smooth silky skin

4 Write the **alliteration** in *Buy Now!* S__________ S__________ S__________

Grammar Rules! Student Book 1 (ISBN 9780655092414) © Tanya Gibb/Matilda Education Australia

5 Write **proper nouns** on the lines to show **alliteration**.

Terrible T__________ tickled T__________ toes.

Lovely L __________ loves lemon lollies.

6 Write **adjectives** on the lines to show **alliteration**.

D__________ Dave draws d__________ dinosaurs.

S__________ Suri stole s__________ Sam's sneakers.

Rule

When two words are joined together and letters are left out, the new shorter word is a **contraction**.
An **apostrophe** shows that a letter or letters have been left out. *I am → I'm*

7 Write two **contractions** used in *Buy Now!* __________ __________

8 Choose the correct **contraction** from the box. Write it on the line.

She's	It's	I'll	You'll

________ (You will) love it.

________ (I will) love it.

________ (She is) going to love it.

________ (It is) slime.

9 Draw a line to link each **contraction** to the full words.

can't	do not
don't	cannot
isn't	did not
didn't	is not

10 Choose one **contraction**. Use it in a sentence.

____

Make up a name for a new food. Use **alliteration**. Create an advertisement to sell your new food.

Grammar Rules! Student Book 1 (ISBN 9780655092414) © Tanya Gibb/Matilda Education Australia

Unit 27

Sensing and thinking verbs, antonyms

Sharks

I think that sharks are really interesting animals. Some sharks, like the grey nurse, are harmless to people. Some sharks, like the great white, can be deadly to people. I believe that some people are unfair to sharks. They want to kill them just because they're sharks. They shouldn't hate sharks so much. People should protect sharks. The health of the ocean depends on sharks. I love sharks.

The writer's purpose is to give an opinion about sharks and try to convince others to accept their opinion.

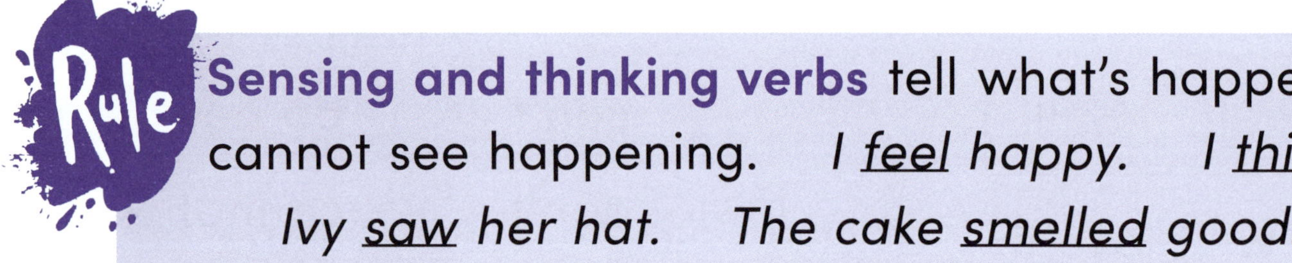

Rule **Sensing and thinking verbs** tell what's happening that you cannot see happening. *I feel happy.* *I think it's cold.* *Ivy saw her hat.* *The cake smelled good.*

1 Read *Sharks*. Find and circle these **sensing and thinking verbs**: *think, believe.*

2 Circle the **sensing or thinking verb** in each sentence.

Shark skin feels like sandpaper.

I think sharks are interesting.

I love sharks.

Do you like sharks?

I hope people protect sharks.

3 Write **adjectives** from *Sharks* on the lines.

Sharks can be ______________ or ______________.

4 What does the writer of *Sharks* want people to do about sharks?

____

Antonyms are words that mean the opposite of each other.

hard → soft *quiet → noisy* *early → late*

5 Find an **antonym** in *Sharks* for each word.

harmful ____________ love ____________

boring ____________ fair ____________

6 Draw lines to link pairs of **antonyms**.

hot	die
fact	ugly
thick	cold
beautiful	thin
live	opinion

7 Write ***un*** in front of each word to make an **antonym**.

happy → unhappy

able → ____________

lucky → ____________

stuck → ____________

likely → ____________

loved → ____________

8 Write your **opinion** about sharks. Give a reason for your opinion. Use **sensing and thinking verbs** for what you think or feel.

____

____

Work with a partner. Write a persuasive text. Tell readers that they should agree with your opinion and why. Use **sensing and thinking verbs.**

This text lists jobs for an imaginary story character, based on the fairy tale *Cinderella*.

Cinderfella's Jobs

1. Quietly clean the chimney.
2. Spotlessly mop the floors.
3. Briskly scrub the toilet.
4. Neatly make the beds.
5. Carefully wash the ball gowns.

1 Read *Cinderfella's Jobs*. Underline the **action verb** in each **command**. Now circle a **noun** in each **command**.

2 Do you think Cinderfella needs to do the jobs in the sequence 1 to 5? Why or why not?

____

3 Which of *Cinderfella's Jobs* would you like least? Why?

____

4 If you had to do one of *Cinderfella's Jobs*, which would you choose? Why?

____

____

Adverbs add meaning to verbs, other adverbs or adjectives. They can tell <u>how</u> to do something.

slowly *very quickly* *really quietly*

5 Write five **adverbs** from *Cinderfella's Jobs* that tell <u>how</u>. ______________________

____

6 Use an **adverb** from the box in each sentence.

happily
slowly
kindly
badly
quickly
angrily

My brother sings ______________.

The fox ran ______________.

The baby played ______________.

The turtle walked ______________.

The dog growled ______________.

The teacher smiled ______________.

La, la, la

7 Write an **adverb** from *Cinderfella's Jobs* on each line.

I ______________ tiptoed past the sleeping tiger.

I wrote the letter ______________.

I ______________ swept the path.

I ______________ tidied my room.

8 Write an **adverb** of your own on each line.

Pat the kitten ______________.

Wash the dog ______________.

Dad sings ______________ in the shower.

My sister chews ______________.

The baby sleeps ______________.

Try it yourself!

Write a list of jobs for a story character, such as Goldilocks or Red Riding Hood. Use **adverbs**.

Reflection

- I can do this.
- I am not sure.
- I need help.

Unit 29 Noun groups, adjectives

Magic Potion

This potion turns baby brothers and sisters into playful puppies.

Ingredients:

- Two snail shells
- Three puppy hairs (any breed)
- 1/2 cup of goblin snot
- One nail clipping from the baby

Method:

1. Mix all ingredients in a small bowl.
2. Place one spoonful of the mixture on the baby's hairbrush.
3. Chant three times, "Playful, peaceful puppy!"
4. Be patient! The potion can take up to five minutes to work.

Warning: This potion only lasts for one hour. To make it stick for more than one hour, add some glue at Step 1.

This recipe is imaginative. Recipes use precise quantities.

Rule A **noun group** is a group of words that includes a noun. A noun group can include an **article**, as well as **adjectives** that describe or tell quantity.

six squealing puppies baby brothers and sisters a few jobs

1 Circle the TWO noun groups in this sentence.

Mix all ingredients in a small bowl.

2 Would you like *Magic Potion* to be real? Why or why not?

____

____

3 Choose the correct **adjective** from the box to complete the noun groups.

Many Some dozen first

_____________ children are away today.

_____________ branches fell from the tree.

I ran in the _____________ race.

Buy a _____________ eggs.

4 Choose the correct **adjective** from the box to complete each noun group.

four six two three eight

A bird has _____________ legs.

A horse has _____________ legs.

An insect has _____________ legs.

A spider has _____________ legs.

Goldilocks annoyed the _____________ bears.

5 Write numbers 1 to 4 in the boxes to sequence the steps.

☐ Cook at 180° for 30 minutes.

☐ Mix ingredients well.

☐ Put spoonfuls of the mixture on a greased oven tray.

☐ Add ingredients to a large bowl.

6 What would be the best things about turning a baby into a puppy?

____

____

Write a **recipe** for a magic potion. Use noun groups. Remember that recipes use precise quantities.

Unit

30 Revision

1 Write 2 to 5 in the boxes to <u>sequence</u> the events in time. Hint! Look at the underlined **time connectives**.

1	We had an assembly today.
	<u>Then</u> it was time to go home.
	<u>Then</u> my brother did a dance.
	<u>First</u> the principal spoke.
	<u>After</u> my brother danced, his class sang songs.

Happy Piggies

- Home for rescued pigs -

Cuddle and feed the pigs.

Wander through our gardens.

We promise you a great day out.

Visit soon!

2 Circle the correct answer or answers.

Happy Piggies is (imaginative/informative/persuasive).

3 What does the writer of *Happy Piggies* want you to do?

____

4 Write an **adverb** from the box on each line.

sadly
madly
happily
noisily
swiftly

Her eyebrows wiggled _______________.

The movie ended _______________.

The teacher smiled _______________.

The bird flew _______________.

The giant thumped _______________.

5 Draw a line to link each **contraction** with the full words.

he's	is not
didn't	you are
they're	that is
that's	they are
isn't	did not
you're	you will
you'll	he is

6 Draw lines to link pairs of **antonyms**.

right	down
tall	little
up	short
give	last
finish	start
big	take
first	wrong

7 Write a **sensing or thinking verb** from the box on each line.

enjoy	loved	think	like	understand

Did you ______________ your dinner?

Do you ______________ problems?

Would you ______________ some more ice-cream?

What do you ______________ about sharks?

I ______________ that story!

8 Choose the correct **adjective** to complete each noun group.

one	four	two	many	some

Strong zebras have ____________ legs.

Some camels have ____________ humps.

A hive has ____________ worker bees.

I'd like ____________ chocolate chip ice-cream.

A whale has ____________ huge tail.

Unit 31 Compound words, quotation marks

This text is informative. It **explains** the life cycle of a silkworm.

Life Cycle

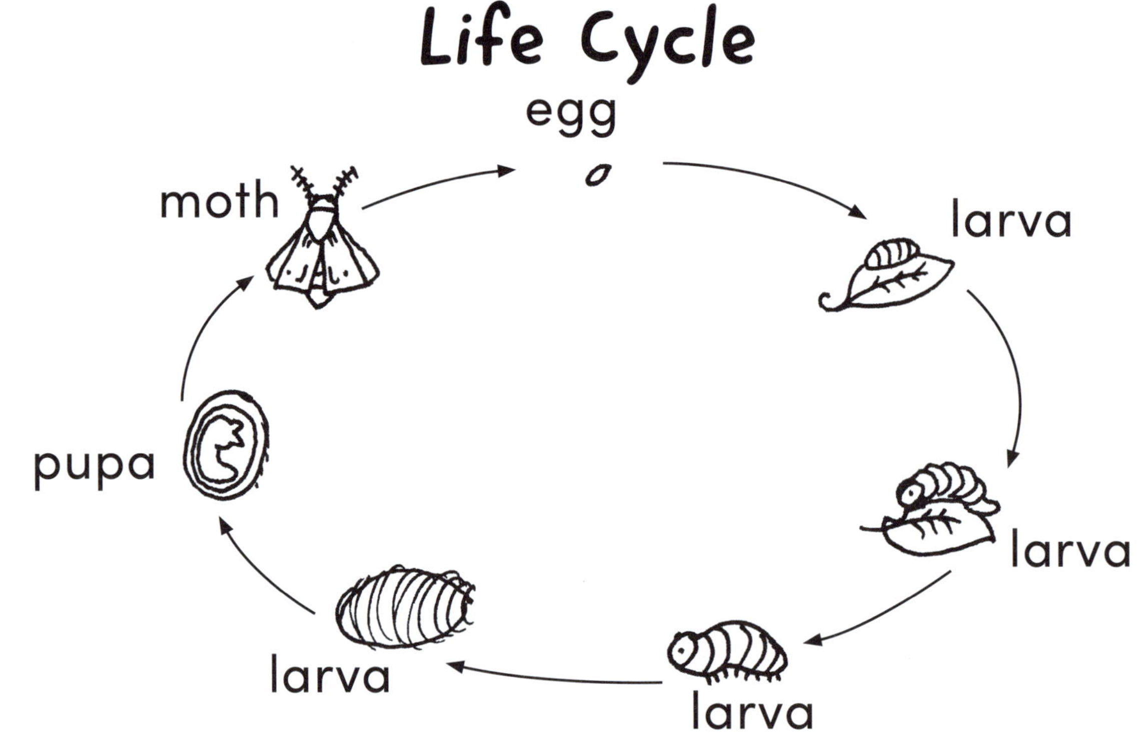

A tiny silkworm larva hatches from its egg. The larva eats mulberry leaves and grows bigger and bigger. As it gets bigger it sheds its skin a number of times. When the larva has grown big enough, it spins a cocoon around itself. Inside the cocoon the larva changes into a pupa with a hard brown shell. After a few weeks a moth crawls out of the cocoon.

Rule Two words joined together make one **compound word**.

foot + ball = football *class + room = classroom*

1 Read *Life Cycle*. Find the **compound word**. ____________

2 Join a word in box 1 to a word in box 2. Write the new **compound words**.

1		
soft	bath	foot
bed	Sun	birth

2		
room	day	day
ball	room	ball

____________ ____________ ____________

____________ ____________ ____________

3 Complete each sentence with a noun group from *Life Cycle*.

______________________________ hatches from its egg.

A pupa has ______________________________.

4 Choose the correct **action verb** from the box. Write it on the line.

eat
shed
lay
hatch

Silkworm moths __________ eggs.

Silkworms __________ mulberry leaves.

Silkworms __________ from eggs.

Silkworms __________ their skin.

5 Write numbers 1 to 4 in the boxes to sequence the events.

☐ The larva spins a cocoon.

☐ A silkworm hatches from its egg.

☐ The silkworm larva eats and grows bigger.

☐ The moth crawls out of the cocoon.

Rule **Quotation marks** are used to show the words that are spoken. *"My silkworms have hatched!" exclaimed Mareka.*

6 Add **quotation marks** to each sentence.

The silkworm moth can't eat because it doesn't have a mouth, said Molly.

It can't fly because its wings are too small, replied Salam.

Choose an animal and find out about its life cycle. Draw a diagram to show the life cycle.

This is an imaginative text. The **directions** help a story character find the way home.

HOW TO GET HOME

- Start at X.
- Walk along the path.
- Go across the bridge. (Beware of the troll under the bridge).
- Turn left at the fork in the path.
- Walk past the gingerbread house.
- Go around the tree. (Don't talk to the wolf behind the tree.)
- Keep walking along the path.
- Stop to help get the cat out of the well.
- Follow the path all the way to the cottage of the bears.

1 Help the little bear get home! Follow the **directions** above. Draw the route for the little bear on the map. Use arrows. → → →

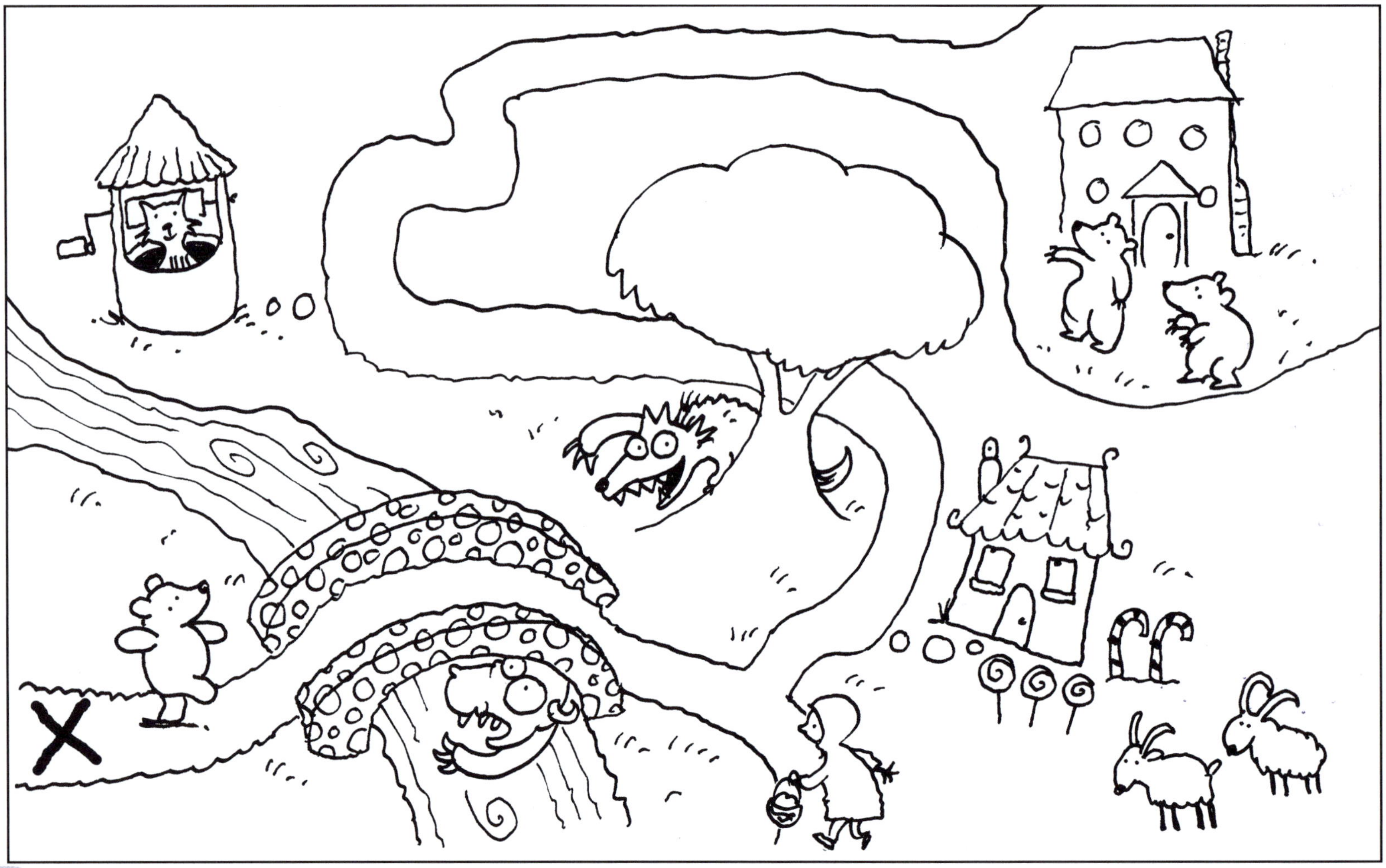

X

2 List the story characters you can see on the map.

___

___

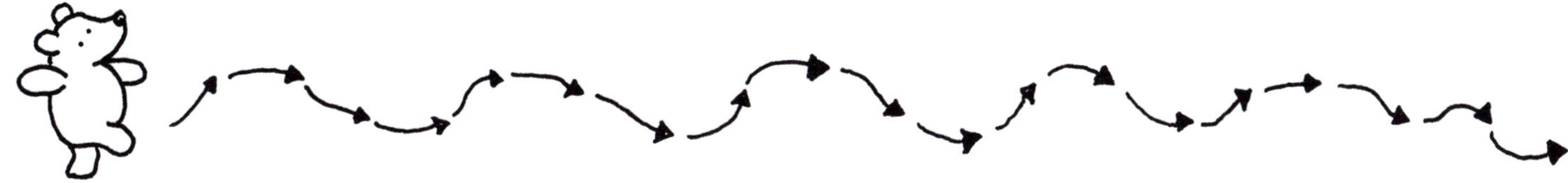

3 Underline the **prepositional phrases** that tell <u>where</u> in *How to Get Home*.

4 Write a **prepositional phrase** that tells <u>where</u> on each line. Use the map in question 1 to get ideas.

The bears waited ___.

The wolf hid ___.

The troll hid ___.

The goats walked ___.

Red Riding Hood strolled ___.

5 Write a **prepositional phrase** that tells <u>where</u> for these things in your classroom.

Paint is kept ___.

Books are stored ___.

The teacher's desk is ___.

The children sit ___.

Draw a map of your school. Choose a secret spot. Write **directions** to tell someone where to find your secret spot. Use **prepositional phrases** to tell <u>where</u>.

Reflection

- I can do this.
- I am not sure.
- I need help.

The writer's purpose is to respond to a book she has read. She gives her opinion and reasons.

Book Review

Student's Name: Lilly

Title: The Bunyip of Berkeley's Creek

Author: Jenny Wagner

Illustrator: Ron Brooks

Comment: At first I thought the story was really sad.

The bunyip kept asking "What am I?" and all the animals said he was a horrible-looking bunyip. The bunyip sighed a long, deep sigh and went back to his waterhole.

But then another bunyip crawled out of the waterhole and asked, "What am I?"

The bunyip yelled, "You're a bunyip just like me!"

The story had a happy ending because the bunyip had found a friend. I really loved this story.

1. Read *Book Review*. Underline the **adjectives** used by the animals to describe the bunyip.

2. What **adjectives** might the bunyip use to describe the other bunyip?

___

3. Write the **question** that the bunyips asked.

___

4 Find a **compound word** in *Book Review*.

____

5 What is Lilly's **opinion** of the story? Write the sentence that tells you her **opinion**.

____

6 Does Lilly's *Book Review* persuade you to want to read the book? Why or why not?

____

7 How might the bunyip have felt when he yelled, "You're a bunyip just like me!"?

____

8 Add **quotation marks** to each sentence to show what is said.

I don't believe in bunyips, said Sebastian.

They are only in stories, commented Mum.

I love stories about bunyips, said Sophie.

Me too, said Sebastian.

9 Add a **verb** of your own to each line.

"I __________ sad for the bunyip," __________ Lilly.

The bunyip __________ a long sigh.

"You __________ a bunyip," __________ the bunyip.

Lilly __________ the story.

Try it yourself!

Write a book review about a book you like or dislike. Use **adjectives** and **sensing and thinking verbs**. Give your **opinions**.

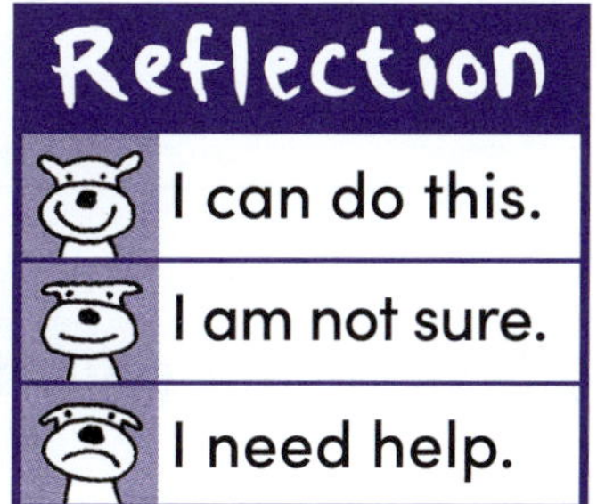

Unit 34

Clauses, verbs, pronouns

The purpose of this report is to inform readers about koalas.

Koalas

Koalas are marsupials. Females have pouches for their babies.

Koalas have thick grey woolly fur. They live in trees and are excellent climbers. They eat eucalyptus leaves. Koalas sleep for 18 to 20 hours a day. They are most active at night.

Male koalas grunt and bellow. Female koalas bellow too, but they also make special sounds for their babies. Females murmur, hum and click. A frightened koala screams like a human baby.

Remember the **saying verbs** rule on page 28.

1 Read *Koalas*. Circle the **verb** in every clause.

2 Write six **saying verbs** used in *Koalas*.

____

3 Write three **adjectives** used to describe a koala's fur.

__________ __________ __________

4 Write the **adjective** that describes a koala's ability to climb. __________

Repeating important words helps a text make sense.

5 In *Koalas*, circle the word *koalas*. How many times is it **repeated**? __________

6 Use a different colour and circle the **pronoun** *they*. How many times is it **repeated**? ________

7 Which noun does *they* replace in *Koalas*? __________________

8 Underline the **relating verbs** in *Koalas*. How many are there? ___________

Copy a sentence from *Koalas* that uses a **relating verb**.

____

9 What does *marsupial* mean? Use a dictionary or ask an adult.

____

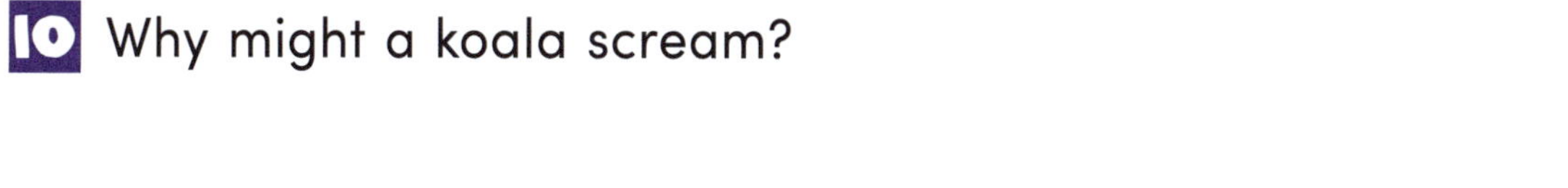

10 Why might a koala scream?

____

____

11 Would you like to be a koala? Why or why not?

____

____

12 Write a **prepositional phrase** that tells where or when on each line.

Koalas live ________________.

They are most active ________________.

Write an **information report** about an animal. **Repeat** the noun for your animal or use **pronouns** to replace the noun. Make sure the report makes sense.

Reflection
I can do this.
I am not sure.
I need help.

Unit 35

Revision

1 Add **quotation marks** to each sentence.

Pick up your socks, said Aunty.

Put your schoolbag away, said Mila.

Wash your hands, said Sara.

I'm going out, said Dom.

2 Circle the noun groups.

We live in a two-bedroom unit. Sasha has nice friendly neighbours.

There are six tiny puppies in the Labrador's litter.

3 Join a word in box 1 to a word in box 2. Write the new **compound words**.

1		
eye	under	high
foot	silk	base

2		
path	wear	ball
way	worm	brow

__________ __________ __________

__________ __________ __________

4 Circle the **verbs** in the sentence.

The bunyip sighed and went back to the waterhole.

5 Write an **adjective** to describe each **noun**.

__________ koala   __________ baby

__________ tree   __________ dad

__________ mum   __________ principal

__________ friend   __________ playground

6 Rewrite each sentence on the line below. Use correct punctuation marks.

where is leos toothbrush asked arlo

____

its on the sink, replied zara

____

ive got it exclaimed arlo

____

7 Write words from the box on the lines.

babies Koalas They make eat trees sleep Female koala

Koalas are marsupials. __________ have thick, grey, woolly fur. __________ live in __________. Koalas __________ for 18 to 20 hours every day. Koalas only __________ eucalyptus leaves. Koalas __________ interesting noises. __________ koalas murmur and hum for their __________. A frightened __________ will scream.

8 Choose the correct **conjunction** from the box. Write it on the line.

and but so because

Goldilocks tried Daddy Bear's porridge __________ it was too hot.

Goldilocks tried Mummy Bear's bed __________ she tried Daddy Bear's bed.

Goldilocks ran away ______________ the bears were coming home.

Baby Bear's chair was broken ____________ Mummy Bear fixed it.

Glossary

Look at the page number in the circle to find more information about the rule or tip.

adjective .... a word that tells more about a **noun** (15)

adverb .... a word that adds meaning to **verbs**, other adverbs or **adjectives**; can tell how to do something (62)

alliteration .... when the beginnings of words sound the same (58)

antonym .... a word that means the opposite of another word (61)

article .... a small word used in front of a noun or at the start of a noun group (41)

character .... who a story is about. Characters are described in specific ways to influence how the reader feels about them (39)

clause .... a group of words that includes a **verb**. A simple sentence is one clause. (17)

command .... a sentence that tells someone to do something (20)

compound sentence .. a sentence that has two equal **clauses** joined by a **conjunction** (25)

compound word .... two words joined together (68)

conjunction .... a word that joins **clauses** (25) (48)

contraction .... a shortened form of a word or words (59)

exclamation .... a sentence that shows strong emotion, like anger or surprise (25)

homophone .... a word that sounds the same as another word but has a different meaning (35)

noun .... a word for a person, place, animal or thing (8)

- **common noun** (8)
- **proper noun** (12)  (14) (46)
- **singular and plural** (36)

noun group .... a group of words that includes a **noun** and other words that tell more about the noun 64

onomatopoeia .... when words sound like the things they represent 57

personal pronoun .... a word that is used in the place of a **noun** 44

possessive apostrophe .... a punctuation mark used to show possession 13

preposition .... a word that begins a **prepositional phrase** 10

prepositional phrase .... a unit of meaning that begins with a **preposition**

a group of words that can tell where 10

a group of words that can that tell when 27

question .... a **sentence** that asks something 34

quotation marks .... marks used to show words that are spoken; also called speech marks 69

rhyme .... when the ends of words sound the same 45

sentence .... a group of words that make a complete message

A sentence must include at least one **verb**. 17

commands 20 ***fact*** or ***opinion*** 53

compound sentence 25 ***questions*** 34

exclamations 25 ***simple sentence*** 25

synonym .... a word that has a similar meaning to another word 39

time connective .... a word that helps sequence information and events in time 23

verb .... a word or word group that tells what's happening in a **clause**

action verb 9 ***saying verb*** 28

relating verb 15 ***sensing and thinking verb*** 60